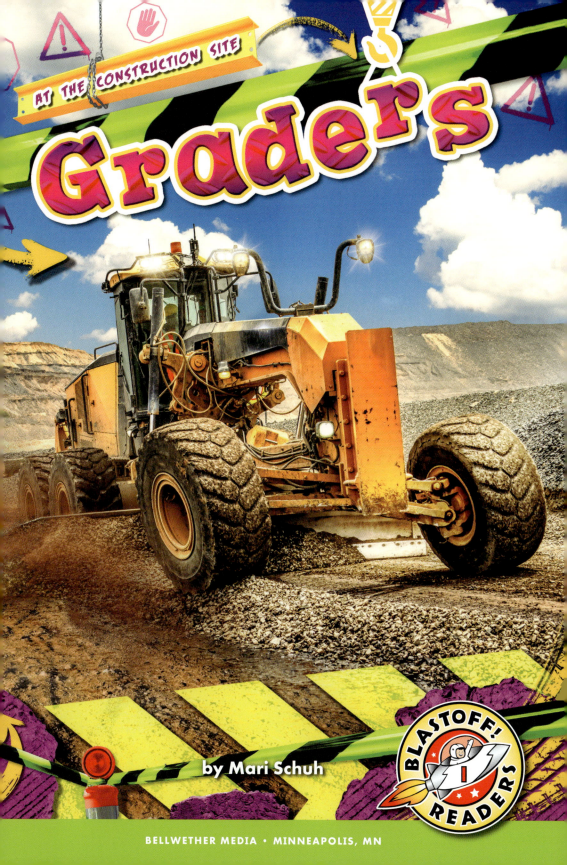

Blastoff! Readers are carefully developed by literacy experts to build reading stamina and move students toward fluency by combining standards-based content with developmentally appropriate text.

 Level 1 provides the most support through repetition of high-frequency words, light text, predictable sentence patterns, and strong visual support.

 Level 2 offers early readers a bit more challenge through varied sentences, increased text load, and text-supportive special features.

 Level 3 advances early-fluent readers toward fluency through increased text load, less reliance on photos, advancing concepts, longer sentences, and more complex special features.

★ **Blastoff! Universe**

This edition first published in 2025 by Bellwether Media, Inc.

No part of this publication may be reproduced in whole or in part without written permission of the publisher. For information regarding permission, write to Bellwether Media, Inc., Attention: Permissions Department, 6012 Blue Circle Drive, Minnetonka, MN 55343.

Library of Congress Cataloging-in-Publication Data

LC record for Graders available at: https://lccn.loc.gov/2024002272

Text copyright © 2025 by Bellwether Media, Inc. BLASTOFF! READERS and associated logos are trademarks and/or registered trademarks of Bellwether Media, Inc. Bellwether Media is a division of Chrysalis Education Group.

Editor: Rebecca Sabelko   Designer: Josh Brink

Printed in the United States of America, North Mankato, MN.

Table of Contents

A Long Grader	4
What Are Graders?	6
Grader Parts	14
Glossary	22
To Learn More	23
Index	24

A Long Grader

A grader moves slowly. It **scrapes** the ground. It pushes dirt as it moves.

scraping dirt

What Are Graders?

Graders are long machines. They are used to move dirt and rocks.

Graders help make new roads. They make the ground flat and smooth.

Graders push snow off roads. They make roads safer for drivers.

Graders make **ditches**. This helps move water away from fields.

Grader Parts

Graders have a long **blade**. It turns and **tilts**. It pushes dirt.

Some graders have two blades. They push a lot of dirt!

Graders can have a **ripper**. It breaks up hard ground.

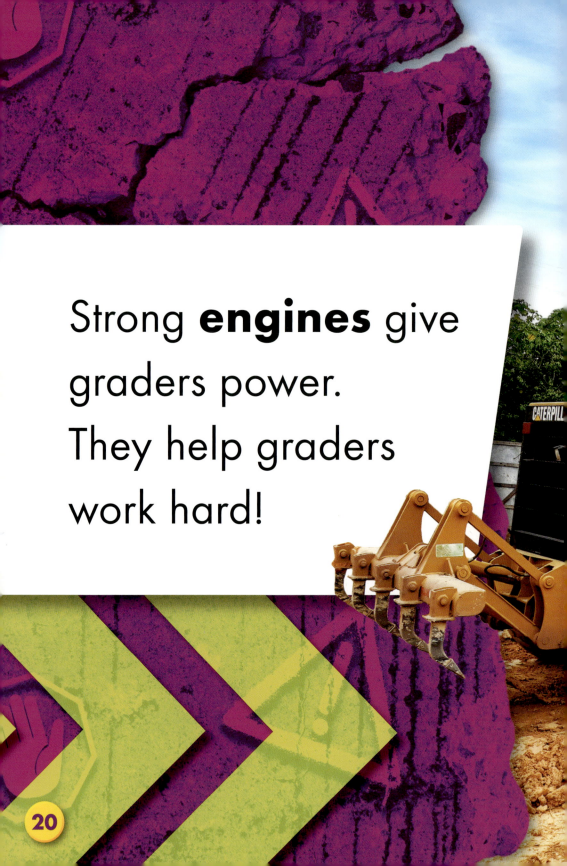

Strong **engines** give graders power. They help graders work hard!

Glossary

blade

a strong, wide part that pushes and flattens dirt

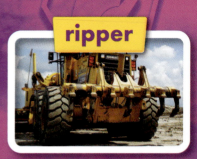

ripper

a sharp tool that breaks up hard ground and rocks

ditches

long, thin areas of land where dirt has been taken away

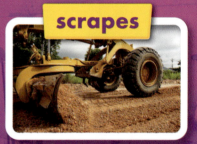

scrapes

moves dirt with a blade

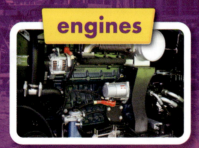

engines

parts that make machines go

tilts

tips to one side

To Learn More

AT THE LIBRARY

Humphrey, Natalie. *Incredible Earthmovers*. New York, N.Y.: Gareth Stevens Publishing, 2023.

Rathburn, Betsy. *Construction Workers*. Minneapolis, Minn.: Bellwether Media, 2025.

Schuh, Mari. *Earth Movers*. Minneapolis, Minn.: Bellwether Media, 2025.

ON THE WEB

FACTSURFER

Factsurfer.com gives you a safe, fun way to find more information.

1. Go to www.factsurfer.com.
2. Enter "graders" into the search box and click 🔍.
3. Select your book cover to see a list of related content.

Index

blade, 14, 15, 16, 17
dirt, 4, 5, 6, 14, 16
ditches, 12, 13
engines, 20, 21
fields, 12
grader jobs, 11
ground, 4, 8, 18
identify, 19
machines, 6
pushes, 4, 10, 14, 16

ripper, 18, 19
roads, 8, 10
rocks, 6
scrapes, 4, 5
snow, 10
tilts, 14
water, 12

The images in this book are reproduced through the courtesy of: Lucian Coman, front cover (hero); Oleg Rebrov, pp. 2-3, 22-24 (background); Mapleman13, p. 3 (grader); chatnarin kongsuk, pp. 4-5; Vadim Ratnikov, p. 5 (scraping dirt); Petr Smagin, pp. 6-7; tracielouise, pp. 8-9; muratart, pp. 10-11; Garmasheva Natalia, pp. 12-13; AlexStreln, p. 13 (grader vectors); Grobler du Preez, pp. 14-15; sky-lord, pp. 16-17; Roman Korotkov, pp. 18-19, 19 (ripper); artemis, p. 19 (blade); Just dance, p. 19 (engine); Josue Carvalho, pp. 20-21; kckate16, p. 22 (blade); Beekeepx, p. 22 (ditches); Orlov Alexsandr, p. 22 (engines); bapake alan, p. 22 (ripper); Love Silhouette, p. 22 (scrapes); Maksim Safaniuk, p. 22 (tilt); Timofeev Vladimir, p. 23 (grader); Red ivory, back cover.